Concord Floral

Also by Jordan Tannahill

PLAYS
Age of Minority: Three Solo Plays
Botticelli in the Fire & Sunday in Sodom
Declarations
Is My Microphone On?
Late Company

FICTION
Liminal
The Listeners

NON-FICTION
Theatre of the Unimpressed: In Search of Vital Drama
The Videofag Book (edited with William Ellis)

Concord Floral

A play by Jordan Tannahill

Playwrights Canada Press
Toronto

LIBRARY AND ARCHIVES CANADA CATALOGUING IN PUBLICATION
Tannahill, Jordan, author
        Concord Floral / Jordan Tannahill.

A play.
Issued in print and electronic formats.
ISBN 978-1-77091-495-7 (paperback).--ISBN 978-1-77091-496-4 (pdf).
--ISBN 978-1-77091-497-1 (html).--ISBN 978-1-77091-498-8 (mobi)

        I. Title.

PS8639.A577C65 2016   C812'.6   C2016-900205-5
                                              C2016-900206-3

Playwrights Canada Press staff work across Turtle Island, on Treaty 7, Treaty 13, and Treaty 20 territories, which are the current and ancestral homes of the Anishinaabe Nations (Ojibwe / Chippewa, Odawa, Potawatomi, Algonquin, Saulteaux, Nipissing, and Mississauga / Michi Saagiig), the Blackfoot Confederacy (Kainai, Piikani, and Siksika), néhiyaw, Sioux, Stoney Nakoda, Tsuut'ina, Wendat, and members of the Haudenosaunee Confederacy (Mohawk, Oneida, Onondaga, Cayuga, Seneca, and Tuscarora), as well as Metis and Inuit peoples. It always was and always will be Indigenous land.

We acknowledge the financial support of the Canada Council for the Arts, the Ontario Arts Council (OAC), Ontario Creates, the Government of Ontario, and the Government of Canada for our publishing activities.

For Andrew

Introduction
Erin Brubacher and Cara Spooner

From 2012–2014, we worked with Jordan as he wrote versions of *Concord Floral*. We made three performances over three years, with ten teenagers from Toronto, Canada, from which Jordan wrote the version of our story that you now have in your hands. We all, in our own ways, grew up with this project, but, in a most literal sense, when we began working together, performers Theo Gallaro, Erum Khan, and Rashida Shaw were thirteen, seventeen, and eighteen years old; by the time we took our original production to one of the largest stages in Canada, they were eighteen, twenty-two, and twenty-three. We owe them thanks, in particular, for being with us throughout that entire journey.

Before this text was taken up by many other companies across Canada and beyond, we co-directed four casts of teenagers in our production in six Canadian communities. Each time we held a first reading of *Concord Floral*, we were reminded of the alchemy of this text and teenage voices: we watched our younger co-conspirators light up as the words left their lips, as they listened to a story they could claim as their own and offer back to us. This was a great honour to witness. We are grateful for a play that allowed us to work in such fine company, and to learn from the hearts, minds, and imaginations of the next generation of artists.

Playwright's Note
Jordan Tannahill

As a teen growing up in the suburbs, my friends and I found refuges for ourselves in the abandoned or underused spaces of our neighbourhood: the oversized parking lots, the vacant bus shelters, the unlit parks and walking paths beyond our backyards. In the summer of 2011 I went to a party at Concord Floral, a million-square foot abandoned greenhouse in Vaughan. Judging from the piles of old cigarette butts, broken beer bottles, underwear, used condoms, and graffiti, I realized that the greenhouse was, and had likely been for several generations, a haven for youthful transgression—much like the ones my friends and I had claimed for ourselves as teens. Around the same time I was reading Giovanni Boccaccio's *The Decameron*, a thirteenth century allegory in which ten youth flee plague-ridden Florence to an abandoned villa in the countryside for ten days. There was such a tangible connection in my mind between this medieval villa and Concord Floral: both were secret hideaways reclaimed by youth as shelters for their stories and coming of age.

I began writing *Concord Floral* as a kind of fantastical portrait of my own neighbourhood, and specifically those liminal spaces adolescents claim for themselves. The suburb I grew up in was both new and quiet, and yet it always carried for me the possibility of myth and magic, of danger and desire. But then perhaps that's just adolescence anywhere.

Concord Floral was written by Jordan Tannahill and developed over a three-year period with Erin Brubacher, Cara Spooner and a group of teenagers from across the Greater Toronto Area. The original production was created and directed by Erin Brubacher, Cara Spooner, and Jordan Tannahill.

Concord Floral was first produced by Suburban Beast and presented by Why Not Theatre at the Theatre Centre, Toronto, from October 12 to 26, 2014, with the following creative team:

Liam Sullivan as 1 (Just Joey)
Troy Sarju as 2 (Bobolink)
Theo Gallaro as 3 (John Cabot)
Melisa Sofi as 4 (Forever Irene)
Jessica Munk as 5 (Rosa Mundi)
Erum Khan as 6 (Nearly Wild)
Sahra Del as 7 (Couch)
Eartha Masek-Kelly as 8 (Fox)
Rashida Shaw as 9 (Greenhouse)
Jovana Miladinovic as 10 (Bobbie James)

Music composition and sound design by Christopher Willes
Lighting design by Kimberly Purtell
Stage management by Laura Hendrickson
Dramaturgy by Erin Brubacher

Characters

1 (Just Joey)
2 (Bobolink)
3 (John Cabot)
4 (Forever Irene)
5 (Rosa Mundi)
6 (Nearly Wild)
7 (Couch)
8 (Fox)
9 (Greenhouse)
10 (Bobbie James)

Notes

In the premiere production, 9 (Greenhouse) announced each chapter number and title. This reinforced her position as narrator and had the effect of repeating the first line of each scene, to sometimes comedic or poetic effect.

The teens never leave the stage. In the premiere production they often stood in a line across the upstage wall, faintly illuminated, witnessing the unfolding action.

Directors should feel at liberty to update pop cultural and geographic references, as well as slang, to fit the production context.

Directors are strongly encouraged to cast actual teenagers from the locale of production.

Prologue

Lights rise slowly.

Fog hovers over a bare stage.

From out of the fog appears 10 (Bobbie James). She appears naked but is too heavily cloaked in shadow and fog to tell for certain.

Somewhere in the distance a chorus of teens can be heard singing a medieval choral piece.

Lights fade slowly to black.

1 //
It was night. We were in a field.

Lights up faintly on a line of TEEN CHORUS *far upstage. Teens 1, 2, 3, 5, and 6 walk downstage.*

2
It was night
We were in a field

3
Behind our houses is this big field
and on the other side—

1
You gotta walk through the field to get to the McDonald's

5
The worst

1
But when you're jonesing for a McFlurry—

2
—you just gotta because otherwise you gotta walk all the way around the highway

6
It's fine if you cut through in a group

1
It was dark

5
Except you get covered in burrs

3
We were supposed to be working on our group presentation

2
For English

6
My life is one big group presentation

1
Everyone came over to my basement

3
But somebody thought it would be a great idea to—

5
I brought the whisky to get the juices flowing

6
Yeah, really helped the brainstorming

1
And then, when everyone was turned

2
Rolo McFlurries, bitches!

3
Was I the only one who even read the book?

6
(indicating with fingers) It's like this big!

5

Hellooo: Wikipedia

1

Just print some shit out and stick it on a bristol board

6

Or a skit

2

I'd rather get the plague

6

Fuck that book

3

Do you even know what the plague is?

5

Your body basically goes inside out

3

The Decameron

6

It's like a thousand years old, moving on

3

A plague comes to Florence and a bunch of teens run away to an abandoned villa

2

What's a villa again?

5

It's like a big house

1
So they just chilled in this big abandoned house?

3
For ten days

6
It's just like us chillin' in Concord Floral

1
In the middle of the field there's this big-ass—

5
—like giant—

1
—abandoned greenhouse

5
Full of broken glass

3
Concord Floral is—

1
It's fuckin'—

2
—sketchballs

6
Kids party in there all the time

3
They got a death wish

1
(indicating 2 and 3) The three of us ran ahead—

6
Rosa and me walked slow, talking about a certain someone—

5
I don't even like him

6
Uh-huh

2
Autumn night

6
I know you're thirsty for him

1
Broken glass in the tall grass

3
The sound of the highway—

2
—like a river

5
He kept trying to make the same joke, did you notice?

6
Yeah that was the worst

5
The others got far away

6
Halfway through the field, I was like, "Screw McFlurries, let's smoke a joint"

5
I'm down

6
(calling to the boys) Hey, we're gonna smoke a J!

5
Can't hear us

6
Screw 'em

5
Here?

6
In the greenhouse

5
Seriously?

6
Are you scared?

5
Not if you aren't

6
We headed out on our own towards the greenhouse

5
It was late
Like ten thirty

6
Quarter after

5
Minimum

6
Concord Floral's been abandoned since like forever

5
Longer than we've been alive

6
Not that long

5
Yeah, for sure that long

6
It's like huge—

5
A million square feet

6
Not that big

5
At least that big

6
Full of rusted metal and—

5
—cigarette butts—

6

—and condoms, which is gross—

5

—but less gross than no condoms, right?

6

Sex ed, people

5

Parents don't even know about it

6

Parents know

5

Mine don't

6

I stole some papers from my brother
but he didn't have weed so can you spot me?

5

Why do you think I'd have any?

6

So you just thought I'd smoke you up?

5

Oh my god, this is so typical

6

How is this typical?

5

Empty promises

6

Why don't we just like grab some of these grasses and smoke them?

5

It won't be, like, at all the same

6

Do you have a better idea?

5

So Nearly and me started walking through the field with our hands out
like this—

    5 and 6 both spread their hands out.

6

—walking with our fingers brushing through the tips of the tall grass
and every once in a while—

5

—just closing our hands like this
and the grass tore from the tips
and came with us until our hands were full of grass—

    Light shift: they have entered the greenhouse.

6

When we got inside the greenhouse I was like
"So you brought the lighter, right?"

5

I thought you brought the lighter

6

You always have a lighter

5

And it's true, I usually do but like—

6

—water under the bridge

5

We started looking around for a lighter in the broken glass—

6

—'cause like kids always leave tons lying around

5

But it was really fucking dark

6

Thank god for the flashlight app

5

Right?

6

Turning over piles of scrap metal—

5

And you gotta be so careful 'cause like every ten feet or so there're these openings—

6

—like wells in the floor—

5

—about this wide

A square of white light appears beside 5.

that drop down like two storeys into the basement
and you can just fall right down and break your neck
So my eyes were to the ground 'cause I didn't want to trip and—

6

—plus we were looking for lighters—

5

I had this thought like: that's what death is like
Just endlessly looking for a light in the darkness
And when I looked up you were so far from me
Like half a football field away
I could just see your little light speck in the distance

6

You were all the way in the caved-in part
where no one goes, where the rain comes through
And then I heard—

5

Shit! Shit! Shit!

6

I looked up and I didn't see anything
just darkness, I was like, "Yo, where are you?"

5

I dropped my fucking phone into one of the wells

6

Where are you?

5

I could see the light glowing down below—

6

And then I heard screaming
Top of her lungs
And I started running towards her
And I followed her screams into the darkness
And when I reached her she was shaking and crying
and I looked down into the basement and saw the light from her phone
And then I saw it

5

A body

6

Of a girl

5

Covered in grass and

6

—mud—

5

Almost buried—

6

—rotting, but not fully

5

—just covered in a pile of sticks and grass

6

—like someone had tried to cover her but ran out of time

5

How do you know it's a girl?

6

Her red sweater

5

It's a girl's sweater

6

The phone's literally—

5

—lying right on top of her

6

I recognize that sweater

5

She's all twisted

6

Maybe she fell in and broke her neck

5

Or was thrown in

6

Who would throw her in?

5

Someone who didn't like her
It's a possibility

6

Murder?

5

Murder is a possibility

6
No, k, but first, let's just figure out—

5
First let's get the fuck out of here

6
Not without your iPhone
that cost like five hundred bucks, your mom will kill you

5
Do you see the body down there?

6
It's your iPhone!

5
There's a fucking body down there

6
She's not going to do anything to you

5
I'll get another one

6
Look—there's a ladder going down into the well

5
No

6
The girl was too injured to climb out

5
How could no one come looking for her?

6

I'm going down

5

Are you insane?

6

It was an iPhone!

5

She climbed into the well

6

There were flies everywhere

5

On the body

6

My face

5

My face

6

I grabbed for the phone—

5 indicates with her hand how the phone slid down the body.

5

—but it slid down the sweater and into the pants—

6

—into the body—

5
—into the space between the sweater and jeans—

6
I can't reach inside

5
But you're so close

6
I'm not reaching in

5
Just one quick move

6
I reached into her body

5
She reached in

6
I can feel it

5
You have it?

6
I think—

5
What if it's her bones?

6
I let go

5

She / started screaming

6

I started screaming

5

—and climbing back up the ladder

6

Inside death

5

Now I was screaming too

6

—top of our lungs, running—

5

—full tilt through the greenhouse—

6

—through the field
through the McDonald's parking lot and—

5

—were practically still screaming when we walked into the McDonald's
and ordered McFlurries

6

Our friends'd already left but we ordered anyway
and just sat there in silence eating
like not even looking at each other—

5

She didn't even wash her hands

6
I was still like totally stunned

5
Traumatized

6
Well—

5
For sure traumatized

6
And we knew what we should do, I mean—

5
We knew we should call the police—

6
—or tell the others, or our parents—

5
That would've been like the—

6
—rational—

5
—responsible thing to do but—

6
—we were just too—

5
Traumatized

6

Plus we would've had to admit to our parents where we'd been
what we'd been doing—

5

So it was just easier—

6

—way easier—

5

For us to just say—

5 & 6

Nothing

5

So we finished our McFlurries and walked home

2 //
This is a play we created for you.

A long line of fluorescent light appears along the lip of the stage.

7
This is a play we created for you

8
About something that happened not long ago

3
In our neighbourhood

2
A neighbourhood not unlike your own

1
Or maybe one you know

9
Personally, I'm better at public speaking than acting, so I'm the narrator
Let's pretend for a second that you are Toronto
And that this line of light is the 407 at night
Let's pretend that this stage is our suburb to the north

7
And our neighbourhood is right about . . . here

A little white square of light appears.

3
And if you zoomed into our neighbourhood like Google Maps—

3 makes a "zoom in" finger gesture; the square of light expands to the entire stage.

—then this would be where my house is

2
And mine

4
And look—

5
Here's mine

6
And this street—

1
At the end of the cul-de-sac is my house and—

7
—across the street

8
—is mine

6
—it's easy to get lost

5
Look

4
—on these streets

7
This is me—

2
Standing on the face of the earth

5
Here I am

4
Look

2
My neighbourhood

3
In my neighbourhood—

5
—a lot of the streets sorta—

3
—we play video games in our basements—

5
—loop back on themselves

1
—we make videos of ourselves—

6
—and ride bikes past dark—

4
—dancing in our bedrooms—

1
Alone

7
I post poems on my Tumblr

2
We steal garbage bags of doughnuts from the Tim Hortons dumpster—

1
—and hit them with baseball bats in the park

2
(miming a bat swing) Boom

7
Look

3
There's a field—

7
—of tall grass

4
—behind our homes

5
Beyond our backyards

8
Look

4
—where we go to bury our secrets

8

—in that field—

7

—to get lost in—

3

—to hide in

4

In that field—

1

Last summer, on my way to bed
I caught my mother holding her mega-mug of tea in her bathrobe
just staring out the kitchen window towards the field
And I was like, "What are you looking at?"
She said they really ought to tear it down
The old greenhouse
She pointed at a spot at the far end of the field, hidden in the brush
You can't really see it in the dark
She said it was a "scourge"
It's been abandoned forever
I told her nothing is forever

2

All parents are a little stupid
They need to make themselves that way or they'll go insane
worrying about all the things they secretly know to be true

8

Where do your children go at night?

2

You think they stay in their beds?

7
The entire night?

1
Even if their bodies are there, under the covers—

8
What about their souls?

2
Have you ever thought about their souls?

1
All the teenagers in the neighbourhood say—

ALL
Good night

1
But really they're running

2
Through the tall grasses

8
Running—

2
Through that field—

8
—to the hidden place—

7
—where the fire burns—

1
—inside—

7
—that makes them like wolves—

8
—all across the neighbourhood—

2
—through the tall grasses—

8
Running

7
Did we have parties?

1
Drugs?

2
Of course there were parties

1
What do you think?

8
Nothing hard—

3
Can I just say—?

2
Of course there were drugs

8
Fucking?

3
Not all of us—

2
Connect the dots

1
Growing up my mother would tell me to stay away from the greenhouse

7
Of course there was some fooling around

1
A scourge

2
What's that?

1
Something ugly—

3
So—

1
—abandoned

3
—it was an aesthetic grievance?

7
My mom didn't care, she knew I went

4
Not ours

3
No way

4
Home by eleven

3
Sharp

7
My mom always picked me up

8
She drove me too

5
My parents—

8
Parents—

6
They're just scared—

5
That we have a place to ourselves

2
Where no one's making you buy shit or quiet down

1
She was always worried about kids starting fires there for some reason
That was her big thing: fires

8
But we did start fires

4
We did more than start fires

Light shift: the greenhouse.

9
It's true
They lit fires in me
And broke beer bottles in me
And left their condoms and cigarette butts and muddy footprints frozen
in time

2
Pink Osianas

3
Bridal Whites

2
Crested Moss

1
Golden Fantasies

2
Himalayan Musk

9
I was once full of roses
Now they've overrun me

3
Amongst the broken glass

1
—and fallen trellises—

9
Grown wild

2
—gardening gloves and shovels—

1
—and hydroponic lights—

3
—drip-line irrigation—

1
—ladders, thermometers—

3
—hoses—

2
—hard hats and rakes

1
And the memory

3
—of a thousand teenagers' bodies

9
I was built in 1951 by the Rosenbergs
Talk about a family destined to be in the flower business
Esther and David were Jewish florists living in Pankow with their two daughters
They survived the war but their daughters didn't
When they immigrated to Toronto they reopened their flower shop

a bustling spot around Glencairn
before deciding to build me in the quiet town of Concord
just north of the highway
But over the years I grew into the largest rose supplier in the GTA
until 1983, when David died and Esther was moved into a nursing home
They never did find a buyer for me
I doubt Esther is still alive
She once said, "When a baby is born we give the mother roses
When she graduates, when she marries, we give her roses
And when she dies we place roses on her grave
Because a life without beauty is unbearable"
I've seen a few decades of kids grow up inside me
First pets buried, first beers drunk, first kisses, virginities lost
I've heard parents say, "Kids take everything for granted these days"
They're lazy, apathetic
But that hasn't been my experience
I know a lot of kids who've endured
Civil wars and famines
These kids are wise
Aware
And they're searching for a little beauty in the world
Because life without beauty is unbearable

The sound of a school bell.

3 //
Did you hear?

Light shift. The teens arrange themselves as if in a classroom.

7
Did you hear?

8
There's a body in the greenhouse

7
Rosa Mundi
Nearly Wild

8
I don't believe them

7
You don't?

8
Rosa's such a faker

7
Just because she said she met Robert Pattinson in grade eight—

8
She said she went to Robert Pattinson's cottage

7
But that greenhouse is so big—

8
She said that her dad was the breeder who invented the Labradoodle

7
Okay, so she can be full of shit sometimes—

8
And why's no one looking for this missing girl?

7
Maybe nobody cares

8
How can a body just be rotting away like a few blocks from our houses?
In our neighbourhood?

1
I didn't even notice they weren't with us

2
Yeah, right

1
Wallahi

2
I looked back and said, "We should slow down," and you were like
"Rolo McFlurries wait for no one!"

1
Yeah, but I didn't know they were in the greenhouse

6
We were sitting in English
and had like nothing prepared

5

I can wing anything

6

All I could think about was the phone lying inside that girl's body

5

The teacher called our group up

6

The phone inside her—like her soul

5

We had to present

3

I had it covered

5

We knew he would

3, at the front of the class, begins to present.

3

The Decameron is a fourteenth-century allegory by Giovanni Boccaccio
During the time of the Black Death
a group of seven young women and three young men
fled from plague-ridden Florence to an abandoned villa in the countryside
For ten days every member of the party told a story
The stories were about the power of fortune
the power of human will
love tales that end tragically
love tales that end happily
clever replies that save the speaker
tricks that women play on men
tricks that people play on each other in general

and examples of virtue
Paintings of *The Decameron* depict the teens playing music to one another
And I started to wonder: What songs might they have played?
I did a little research on ye olde YouTube
and found a fourteenth-century dance song from northern Italy called "Trotto"

Fourteenth-century "Trotto danza" begins to play.

This is basically like the club music of the Middle Ages
You can imagine the ten teenagers
drinking, dancing, flirting to this song

5
(whispers to 6) Stop staring at me

6
I can't help it

5
Did you tell anyone?

6
No

5
No one?

6
Just my sister

5
Christ

6
She's discreet

5

I feel like everyone in the school knows
When the bell rang I bolted

6

She didn't even save me a spot in the caf

> *The school bell rings. Light shift. The cast arrange themselves as if in
> a cafeteria.*

10

I guess you could say my parents are hippies
Not like fire spinners or naturopaths but like . . .
they have master's degrees in sustainability from Trent
They made me read Milton and Whitman
and didn't trust teachers to do as good a job with their kids
They said I had a very special mind that needed nurturing
So I was home-schooled
I hated it, I was so lonely
I would sneak away sometimes at lunch
and watch the other kids eat in the cafeteria
Finally my parents said, "All right, fine, we'll enrol you in grade nine
But you're going to be bored"
And it's true
I was bored
But I loved it, every minute
No one talked to me
But I loved watching them, sitting with them, pretending, no, not pretending
really being just another kid eating in the cafeteria
I watched them laugh and shout at each other from across the room
I'd watch them eat
It's a loud cafeteria, so no one noticed me
I think eating is a very tender thing
When we were apes some of us would stand around and guard while the
others ate

Because that's when we are most vulnerable
It's the time we are most tender with each other

Light shift.

1
After school I headed home to watch TV

2
After school

6
She just cut

5
I went to the mall

6
Didn't even wait for me

4
After school

5
I had to get a new phone

6
You said we'd pick it out together

5
We had a secret

2
I went home and made a YouTube video of myself shaving

5

People were staring at me all day

4

I went home and took a shower

6

Fine, fuck your phone

5

Fuck you

4

Before my mom and my brother got home
I rinsed my whole body
Shampooed my hair
And I lay down in the bathtub
and slowly brought the shower head between my legs

6

We promised we would stick together

4

I closed my eyes

6

I was freaked out

4

And brought the nozzle closer
Started thinking of my classmates

6

I tried imagining the face of the girl

4
Imagined each one of their faces

6
In that hole

4
The way they smile

6
What her face would look like with skin

4
The gaps between their teeth

6
The colour of her eyes

4
Their smell

6
The colour of her hair

4
Their haircuts

6
Her sweater

4
Sometimes I like to imagine what they are going to be like when they're all grown up
Living in their houses with their husbands and wives when they let themselves go

6

I felt like I was going to throw up all day

4

Or how it would feel to be pregnant

6

And then I got home and I did
I puked

4

To have a life in you

6

My mom was like, "You're not pregnant, are you?"
I was like, "Oh my god, Mom, fuck off"
and went up to my room and slammed my door

4

I was so deep into it that I lost track
and suddenly I heard my mom and brother arguing outside the bathroom
and they burst in and I was just lying back
with the shower head between my legs
and my mom said, "What on earth are you doing?"
as if she didn't know what on earth I was doing—

3

And I was like, "Wow"
"didn't need to see that, thank you very much"

4

I shouted at them to get out but they just kept standing there
so I jumped up and let go of the shower head
and it began spraying water everywhere
and my mom started yelling and I pushed past them
and ran down the stairs and out the back door

and I lay face down in the backyard crying
and tried to flatten myself until I disappeared
like this
I kept lying there naked until I heard my dad start the lawn mower
He started with the mower at one end
and I knew he didn't know I was there
I lay there, listening to the mower getting closer and closer to me, thinking
"It's okay, Dad will see me in the grass"
closer and closer and closer until the sound of the mower's so close
I jumped up screaming and my dad's right beside me
and he screamed, all startled
He hadn't seen me
I looked him right in the eye and I knew:
he would've run over me
And cut my face right off
I would've had no face
A freak with no face

3
I came out and I handed her her clothes

4
Thanks

3
Mom's pissed

4
It was nothing

3
She's soaked

4
She deserved it

3

You're sick

4

Men like to make women feel that way

3

You're my sister

4

So?

3

I'm going inside

4

Did you hear about the body?

3

What body?

4

Two girls found a body at Concord Floral last night

3

What?

4

At least that's what they said

3

What kind of body?

4

A human one

3
Like—

4
A girl

3
Where'd they find it?

4
I told you, at Concord—

3
But where?

4
How should I know?
It's probably not even true

    Pause.

Well, if someone was to find a body around here it would probably be there
Wouldn't it?

    Light shift.

4 //
I'm learning to get better.

Box of light appears on 1.

1

I'm learning to get better
At a lot of things
Knowing more about the world
Capitals and countries
How to dress
How to take better selfies
I post a selfie and it gets thirty-five likes in ten minutes
Monday at four o'clock: that's prime time for likes
Then I take a few cock pics and post them on Craigslist
19-year-old 7-inch, brown hair, hazel eyes
Looking to hook up nearby, can't host, healthy
Looking for 18–30 but open to older if you're hot
No chubs, not too hairy
No creepers or pic collectors
Serious for 2nite
Will bottom for the right guy
I get twenty-four replies in the first hour
Mostly weirdos
A few guys living downtown
Students
Potheads
A twinky skater
Can't tell if he's real
The second I tell them I'm living in Vaughan they're like, "Forget it"
Or just don't reply
I'm like—it's just an hour on the TTC
I'd ride an hour for a blow job, wouldn't you?
Maybe they get lots

Maybe it's just like a bowl of cereal if you live downtown
And then around midnight I start a back-and-forth with a guy from Vaughan
"Are you really nineteen?"
"Ya, you?"
"Thirty-five"
"You wanna get sucked off?"
"Do you bottom?"
"Maybe"
"Have you bottomed before?"
"Not really"
"Lol, you don't know?"
"I can't host"
"Neither can I"
"I can give you head in your car. Or a park?"
·"What about Concord Floral? You know it?"
"The greenhouse?"
"Meet you there in an hour?"
I'm like, "Um, okay, but bring condoms" and he's like, "Lol k k"
He isn't thirty-five
He's probably forty-five
Maybe fifty
I know him
He's the dad of a kid in my school, a grade younger
I've seen him shovelling his driveway in his suit some mornings
He has grey on his temples
In the dark of the greenhouse his cock is in shadows
but I can tell it's huge, veiny
I imagine him fucking his wife with it
I don't know if I should ask him to put a condom on
I don't want him to think I don't know what I'm doing
and maybe I'm not doing it right,
am I supposed to be blowing or is it just sucking
why isn't it called a suck job, and how should I be:
crouched down or squatting or kneeling?
It hurts to kneel on the broken glass—

and then all of a sudden he comes
He just grunts and I feel it in my mouth
and I stand up and spit it out
and like I'm still totally dressed
and as he's zipping his fly I notice these two eyes
glinting by the door of the greenhouse
A fox
I think it was watching us
The guy turns around and the fox darts into the field
"Hope he doesn't tell anyone," he chuckles

 A fox enters.

8
It's true, I was watching them
People think animals don't understand what sex is
Maybe a cat doesn't
But dogs do
Foxes do
My issue is this is where we have sex
I have sex in the greenhouse
Humans, they have thousands of places to have sex
They build whole rooms for it
Why do they need more?
Why do they need to take ours?
Humans feel entitled to everything
They think theirs is the only story
The only romance

1
When I get home I have a shower
And then jerk off twice before heading to bed
Sometimes I feel insatiable
It's difficult to explain
I saw him a week or so later raking leaves

I was waiting for the bus
He looked right at me but didn't recognize me
Or if he did, he didn't let on

Light shift.

5 //
Nearly spent like six hours Facebooking.

A box of light appears on 6.

6

I spent like six hours Facebooking until my parents went to bed
When it was quiet I crept downstairs to get a glass of water
I kept looking out the window expecting something
The street was empty
Each time
Nothing
Just the sound of the neighbour's dog barking in the next yard

A box of light appears on 4.

4

That's my dog

6

How come you never let him in?

4

He pees on the couch

6

I was just about to crawl into bed when my phone buzzed

A box of light appears on 5.

5

Hey guys here's my new number
xoxo Rosa

6

I added it to my contacts and put the phone down
And then it started to ring

6's cell begins to ring.

It was her old number
It was a call from Rosa's old number
I didn't answer

6's cell stops ringing.

I started to shake
I called Rosa's new number

6 puts the cellphone to her ear.

Rosa, someone's got your phone

5

What?

6

Your old phone
Someone just tried to call me

5

Are you messing with me?

6

For real

5

I cancelled the contract

6
How would they even, like—?

5
—climb down and pull it out of the bones

6
—of her ribs

5
No way

6
She was completely hidden

5
Well, we found her

6
I'm fucking freaked out
Should I text back?

5
Yes

6
And say what?

5
How did you get my friend's phone?

6
(texting into phone) There

5
Anything?

6
Not yet

5
Anything?

6
Just wait

5
I hate waiting

6
Just—

    6 begins to sort of hyperventilate.

5
What?
What is it?

6
—oh my god, oh my god—

5
Tell me

6
"She dropped it in me"
That's what it says

5
Someone's fucking with us

6
I don't know

5
It's Just Joey

6
What should I do?

5
Or one of those guys

6
But it doesn't make sense
How would they even get the phone?
Rosa?

5
I'm thinking

6
Stay on the phone with me?
Please?

> *Lights dim on 5 and 6 as they sit on their phones in silence. A box of light appears on 4. She has been watching.*

4
The light was on in her window
I watched it all night long from my room
Across the backyard
She can't sleep
Maybe there really is a body in the greenhouse

> *The lights slowly fade on 4 as she watches, and rise again on 5 and 6.*

6
Are you still there?

5
Yeah

6
What are you doing?

5
Same thing I was doing two minutes ago

6
Lying in bed?

5
No, I'm water-skiing

6
What colour is your new phone?

5
I already told you, it's black

6
Right

5
There's like no selection at Grand Mall

6
Can you hear that girl's dog barking?

5
On your phone

6
So annoying

5
Animal cruelty

6
Totally
They should tie her up in the backyard and see how she likes it

Beat.

God, that's a sick thought, isn't it?
Does your mind ever do that sometimes?
Go to a real sick place?
I can't help myself sometimes
Punishing people like that
It's a real old-fashioned way of being, isn't it?
Like that book from class—
Everyone is dying of the plague 'cause
God is punishing them
The Angel of Death moving over the town
It's just like a horror movie
You do something bad—
like have sex in a hot tub with your best friend's boyfriend—
well, you're going to get the plague
You know?
Or be drawn and quartered
Rosa?
You still awake?

5 turns off her cellphone. Lights only on 6.

I lie in bed
But I can't sleep
It feels like something in the air has shifted
Like something's about to happen
I hear the furnace in the basement turn on
The warm air moving through the house

6's cellphone rings. She hesitates. She answers it.

Who are you?

A light up faintly on 10.

10
You know

6
No

10
I'm Bobbie

6
How did you get her phone?

10
It's inside me

6
What?

10
You want me to show you?

6
How?

10
I'm in your backyard

6
What?

10

You can't see me
But I'm looking at your window

    6 walks to the window and holds up her fist.

6

How many fingers am I holding up?

10

None

    6 begins to cry.

Nearly?

6

Go away

10

I need your help

6

I'm tired, I'm—

10

Please

6

You want me to call the police?

10

Tell them you got a call from a dead girl?

6

Why you calling me?

10
Because you're the one who knows

*6 ends the call. She immediately dials 5. Lights up on 5 again, in
her bedroom.*

5
Hey, sorry I fell asleep—

6
She was in my backyard

5
What?

6
Bobbie

5
Who's—?

6
The girl from the greenhouse

5
The bones—?

6
She called me on my fucking cell

5
I thought you said she was—

6
I asked her where she was, and she said she was standing in the backyard
but I couldn't see her and I held up my hand in the window

and asked her to tell me how many fingers I was holding up
but I wasn't, I was just holding up my fist, and she said none
She said no fingers, Rosa, no fingers

5
K

6
Hello?

5
Yeah?

6
Aren't you totally freaked out?

5
This joke was like—not funny an hour ago

6
Listen, I know it sounds crazy but I was talking to her

5
Okay

6
You don't believe me

5
I just don't think we should be making fun of this

6
No, this is for real, I swear to you
You don't believe me?
Come over
I'll prove it to you

5
Right now?

6
Right now
I'll call her

5
It's three thirty in the morning

6
Rosa, if you love me, you'll come over
I'm fucking losing my mind

5
I don't know

6
It's two blocks

5
I'm not leaving my room

6
Fine, I'll come over to your house

5
And then—

6
—we'll call her

5
Bobbie

6

And I'm going to give you the phone
And you're going to talk to her

5

Are you really coming over?

6

I'm already putting on my shoes

Light shift. 6 is now in 5's bedroom.

Isn't this fucked up?

5

I don't know what to believe

6

Believe this

6 dials 5's old cellphone number. The phone goes to an automated message.

AUTOMATED VOICE

The number you have dialed is no longer in service
Please hang up and try your call again

6

What the hell? I must've—

6 dials the number again. The same message is heard.

5

I think you should go
I'm really not having any fun anymore

6
Rosa—

5
Please

6
What if we—?

5
I want to sleep

6
—just tried to find—?

5
No

6 exits.

6 //
John is a birdwatcher.

3

I'm a birdwatcher

9

His favourite bird is the bobolink
He grew up taking long walks with his dad in my field
watching for the great blue herons and the yellow warblers with their binoculars
And on some mornings, if they woke early enough,
they would catch sight of the yellow-collared bobolink
with its black-and-white feathers perched on top of me

3

I'm not a NIMBY
Not in my backyard?
I resent when people call me that
I'm just a kid who cares about birds
I don't know if you've heard, but they're tearing down the greenhouse
in the near future
A developer has bought the land, and they're planning on building a
Cineplex
A real full-throttle entertainment centre with an arcade and a food court
But the field, the greenhouse, they're part of the Don Watershed
it's all a protected habitat for migratory birds
scarlet tanagers, rose-breasted grosbeaks
The bobolink
It's hard going door to door if you're not selling cookies
People open the door with the chain on and say
"No thanks, we just had our shutters painted" or
"Do you really believe only 144,000 people go to heaven?"
And people have no problem signing up for raffles or draws

but ask them to sign a petition, no way
All they want is free crap
Cars and vacations or even just a bottle of Vitaminwater,
they'll take whatever they can get
One woman, she said I was doing something good
because birds can't speak for themselves
And I said, "Birds are talking all the time,
we just aren't paying attention"

2 enters as a bobolink.

2
I was away
And then I came back
I was born in this field, but I left when I was very young
I flew back because this place is in my blood
We always come back to the place we started from
In some way or another
My parents were born in this field, and so were their parents
and their parents before them
I don't really consider myself political
but I have to say if they put a big Cineplex here things are going to change
In a big way
In a way that can't be undone
If this field goes I don't know where I'll find a mate
A bird to settle down with and have kids
Well, we won't really settle down,
we'll be flying a lot, but my kids—
they won't know this place
Not like I did, and my ancestors did
But everything changes
You can't avoid that
We find new homes
New ways of being
We haven't much time on earth
Relatively speaking

But life is infinitely beautiful because of, not in spite of, death
And you might think, "Oh, he's awfully young to think about death"
Well, I can tell you, bobolinks do not live very long, not long at all

Light shift.

7 //
Rosa ignored Nearly all next morning like ice cold.

The teens arrange themselves in the cafeteria. The sounds of a bustling lunch hour.

5
I ignored Nearly all next morning like—

7 & 8
Ice cold

9
At lunch Rosa sat with the other girls

5
I don't know why she's messing with me

7
I can't believe she went over to your house—

8
—at four in the morning

6 picks up her cell.

5
Look, she's pretending to get a call

7
How do you know she's pretending?

5
I didn't hear it ring, did you?

7
Maybe it was on vibrate

5
She's totally faking it

6
(into cell) I'm not answering your fucking calls

10
You just did

6
Because I need to know I'm not crazy
My friend thinks I'm pranking her
or that I'm losing my mind

10
Are you?

6
Who are you?

10
Bobbie

6
I don't remember—

10
You don't want to

6
I don't want to talk to you

10
Then hang up

6
You're nothing
You're not a thing

10
Then you're talking to yourself

6
Fuck off

10
She's being cruel to you

6
What?

10
Rosa

6
I'm not talking with you about—

10
Ignoring your texts
Sitting there, talking about you with those girls

6
Shut up

10
It takes almost nothing
To be on top and then the bottom

6
They could bleed from their eyes for all I care

10
Would you?

6
What?

10
Care
If they started bleeding from their eyes

6
They're not going to

10
If you could make them

6
I can't

10
What if I could?
Would you want me to?

6
Make them bleed?

10
Yes

6
You couldn't

10
Who says?

6
I don't believe you

10
You don't?

6
No!
Don't
I'm not a bad person

10
No?

6
No

10
Do you believe I exist?

6
Leave me alone

10
Not until you help me

6
I don't believe in ghosts or voices or hauntings or whatever the hell you are
I don't, and / I can't help you

10
Do you see the girl sitting alone across the cafeteria?

6
Yeah

10
In ten seconds she is going to collapse and have a seizure

6
What?
How do you know—?

10
She will fall to the ground convulsing

6
Will she die?

10
If someone catches her head she won't
But if she hits her head against the concrete she will
Not right away
But several hours later from internal bleeding in the brain

6
But what if—

10
Go!

6 drops her phone and bursts across the stage just as 4 collapses—and her head falls into 6's hands. The rest of the cafeteria freezes in suspended animation.

4
(rapid-fire) Are you afraid of death?
Yes!
Do you believe in heaven?

No
Do you believe hell is other people?
No
Are you spoiled?
Yes
Are you bored?
No
Are you wise beyond your years?
Yes
Do you despair for the future?
No
Do you cry alone sometimes?
Yes
Often?
No
Are you lying?
Yes
Do you think boys are smarter than girls?
No
Are you often lonely?
Yes
Do you wish you were more attractive?
No
Do you wish you had a boyfriend?
Yes
Do you wish you had a girlfriend?
Yes
Do you wish you would masturbate less?
No
Do you have an enemy?
Yes
Do you wish ill on them?
Yes
Do you still have nightmares?
Yes
Do you wish you were a different height?

Yes
Race?
Yes
Gender?
No
Specics?
Yes
Dolphin?
Yes
Monkey?
Yes
Dog?
Yes
Bulldozer
Yes
Submarine
No
Why not a submarine?
I don't like the water. The cool black rushing—
But you said yes to dolphin
Yeah, but they're more free than a submarine
How?
They have willpower
And they know how to laugh
Never underestimate the power of a good laugh!

4 laughs. The cafeteria bursts back into life; the teens scream and jump up from their chairs in reaction to 4's seizure. General chaos ensues as 6 continues to hold 4's head.

8 //
Nothing's wrong with Nearly.

Teens 1, 2, 7, and 8 are shooting the shit in a basement.

1
Nothing's wrong with Nearly

8
She fucking merked that girl

7
Burst across the caf

8
She charged her, yo

2
Knocked her right off her chair

8
Did you see how she was shaking?

7
The teachers had to take her away

2
You hear about her showing up in Rosa's room at like four in the morning?

1
Yeah

2
And talking on her cell talking to nobody—

1
All right—

7
I think she's lost it

2
From finding that body

1
You don't really believe that, do you?

Lights suddenly up on 6 speaking into her cellphone.

6
What do you want?

10
You did a good thing

6
Everyone's posting shit about me
Saying I'm crazy
Ever since you started—
What do you want from me?

10
The truth

6
About what?

10
What happened to me

6

How's that my problem?

10

You've felt it
In the stillness at night, as you lay awake
The shadow you can feel creeping around you

6

Right now?

10

You feel it

6

A shadow—

10

The one that makes you run up the stairs
when you turn the lights off in the basement

6

It's you

10

And your friends
The ones there that night
They feel it too
Growing darker
Moving over the neighbourhood
Like a—

6

—plague

10

The weight of their conscience
They know
The ones who were there

6

That night

10

My body in the hole

6

But what can we do now?
I mean, after all this time?

10

Go back

6

Back?

10

To the greenhouse

6

You want us to go back?

10

And come to terms—

6

—with—

10

—what you did

6
But then you'll leave us alone
Bobbie?
Then you gotta promise to leave me alone
I know things ended real bad for you
but I've got a life to live, okay?
You want me to bring them to the greenhouse?
Bobbie?
Don't leave me alone
Please
We'll go back
I'll go, okay?
I'll go and I'll take them back, okay?
Bobbie?

Lights transition back to the basement.

8
Whatever, she's dead to me

7
Was she even alive to you?

8
We were friends

7
Facebook-style

2
I literally have no idea what it feels like to be dead

7
When you're dead there's nothing
You're just all alone

8
Like Bessarion Station

2
Yo, man, death is Bessarion Station

8
I think my peak was 2012
Grade seven

7
If I wasn't so busy living my life I would probably be like—

8
Sometimes I have this vision of my life where I'm fat and naked
and walking an alligator around on a leash in some strip club in the Nevada
desert

1
My mom is dying

2
What?

7
Your mom is dying?

1
Yeah

2
From what?

1
C. *difficile*

7
From what?

1
She got it in the hospital

7
How?

1
Just surfaces
In the hospital

2
What kind of surfaces?

1
There's a thousand kind of surfaces

7
Everything's a surface

8
Your face is a surface

7
The earth

8
The earth's a surface

2
But, wait, she's like for real dying?

1
Yeah

2
I'm so sorry

1
Yeah

7
Like how long's she got?

1
There's still time

2
Wait, *what* does she have?

1
It's from a spore

2
Like a—?

1
Could've been floating

2
—mushroom?

1
No, no, microscopic

8
Obviously

1
Just accidentally ingested it

2
Like in the food?

1
Any which way

2
So this spore—

1
I have to give her my shit

7
Nah, when she dies she gives you *her* shit

1
No, I mean I have to give her my actual shit

2
What?

1
The doctors want to take my shit and put it inside her

2
Like—

1
In her—

2
Ass?

1
No, her—

2
Stomach?

1
Colon

7
Gross

1
For the bacteria

7
Gross

2
Shut up

8
It's called a fecal transplant

1
Exactly

2
You know about these things?

8
Yeah I know about these things

1
The antibiotics she was taking?
It killed all the bacteria in her gut that normally would fight the *C. difficile*
So she needs my good bacteria to save her

7

Wow

2

Intense

1

Yeah

8

Hope you're working up a big turd

1

I've been like constipated for three days

8

Performance anxiety

Silence.

1

I should get Nearly to donate

7

Why?

1

She seems pretty full of shit

They all laugh.

8

Honestly: after all this bullshit?
Nearly's just like whatever, she's dead to me

7
Not *dead* dead

8
Kinda

2
Yo: insensitive much?

8
I'm just saying, next time I see her I'm going to be like—

6 suddenly appears in the basement. 7 notices her first.

7
(to audience) And then I swear to god I looked up
and Nearly was just standing there in the basement
We all jumped up—

The reclining teens jump to their feet.

—and I was like, "Oh. My. God"

1
What the hell are you doing here?

6
I'm sorry I—

1
How did you even—?

6
The door was unlocked and I thought—

2
You just walked in?

8
What the fuck, Nearly?

6
We always chill here

1
This is my house

6
I know

1
I didn't invite you

6
Do you guys feel it?

8
I'm not feeling you

6
The plague

7
What?

6
You might not feel it now but you will
Like a shadow, passing over
Her name is Bobbie
The girl from the greenhouse
Don't pretend you don't know

I know you all know so there's no point in pretending
Grade nine
We need to deal with it
And if not for you then for me, just—
Because she's not going to let me be at peace until we set things right
So that's why, I know it's late and cold
But that's why we need to all go back to Concord Floral

1
What?

6
Tonight, if possible
The sooner the better
It's already started
Can you feel it?
She's not going to let any of us rest until we do

    Beat.

So what do you say?

8
(to 1) You're right

1
What?

8
We should shove her up your mom's ass

9 //
What the hell are you doing in my backyard?

A box of light appears on 5 and 6.

5

What the hell're you doing in my backyard?

6

I'm glad you came down
I was running out of stones

5

I thought you were going to break my window

6

I need to tell you—

5

I need to tell you my parents will flip if you don't get out of here
It's like eleven thirty
On a school night

6

Since when have you cared about eleven thirty on a school night?

5

Have you lost it?

6

It's about Bobbie

5

Enough

6
We know her

5
Let it go

6
She won't let me be
Not until we come to / terms with what happened—

5
Nearly

6
And none of us will sleep until we do

5
Why, 'cause you'll keep throwing rocks at their windows?

6
Because her in that hole—

5
Listen—

6
We need to go back to the greenhouse

5
What happened to Bobbie / is not our problem—

6
It's all of our problem
It's going to plague us

5

Well, you go set up a tent in the greenhouse
and if I break out in boils I'll come out to meet you
Until then, leave me the fuck alone, k?

Light shift. 4 watches from her bedroom window.

4

I watched her from my bedroom window
She wasn't sleeping
Neither was I
Everyone seemed restless
I thought, "Well, if I'm not sleeping I might as well go for a walk"
I walked through the field all the way to Grand Mall
It was deserted
Except for a boy
Laying in the middle of the parking lot

(to 1) Did you fall?

1

I can't sleep

4

Neither can I
Aren't you worried about getting hit by a car?

1

At midnight?

4

I heard people deal drugs here at night

1

Is that why you're here?

4
Is that why you're here?

1
I'm waiting

4
For what?

1
Something's coming
Can't you feel it?

4
Yeah

1
Like a shadow passing over the neighbourhood

   Beat.

4
It's stupid
If you think about it

1
What?

4
Grand Mall
It's just a strip of outlet stores
It's not a mall, and there's nothing grand about it

1
But that's the way things are around here
Things are named after things they're not

Like I live on Pine Ridge Way, but there's no pines and there's no ridge
You're the girl from the caf who had the—

4
Yeah

1
Are you okay?

4
Yeah

1
When I was in grade five my friend started shaking like really hard in his desk
He fell to the floor and people were screaming
And the teacher, man, he was so stupid he didn't know what to do
He just stood there making all these phone calls
instead of like, I don't know, picking him up
Eventually some paramedics came
They gave us like a two-hour recess so we were outside
My friend died
Our teacher described it to us the next day as a "Grand Mall Seizure"
I remember I had this image of him and me
running into all the stores with guns and seizing Grand Mall
We would have a list of demands
Like no more naming things after stuff they're not
It made it seem better somehow
To think that while he was shaking on the floor
he was actually knocking over racks of jeans in Old Navy
and toppling piles of shoes in Aldo

Pause.

What does it feel like?

94

4
Sometimes I know it's coming all day
A shadow building in the distance all around me
Just out of sight
A bit what it feels like now
all over the neighbourhood

> *10 faintly appears at the far end of the parking lot, almost imperceptibly lit.*

1
What's that?

4
Where?

1
At the far end of the parking lot
Is it a person?

4
It's watching us
Hey!

1
Don't—

4
What?

1
I'm scared

4
(calling) Is somebody there?

Beat.

I think—

1
What?

4
I think it's here
The thing you were waiting for

1
I don't feel good about this—

4
Let's get outta here

> *1 and 4 run off. A grid of bedrooms appear on stage. The cast each lie in their respective bedrooms. An ambient tone is heard.*

9
Something was passing over the neighbourhood
Like an Angel of Death

> *Blackout. During the following monologues—delivered in darkness—flashes of light reveal 10 passing through the bedrooms of the neighbourhood.*

1
I run home full tilt from the parking lot
Lungs burning, up to my room three stairs at a time
The burn spreading
My skin, just below the skin
A dark pink flesh burn
She's coming
Lights off, under the covers, and I know she's there

I can see her face
In the darkness: she has my friend's face
The moment before he fell to the ground shaking
And a flash again
and she has my mother's face,
who I know can't be saved
for all the love and the shit in the world
The face of all the people I love but can't help
I can't help you, you hear me?
It's not my fault, Bobbie James
So leave me alone!

7 & 2
In a flash

TEEN CHORUS
I saw a girl

3
We all had the same dream

8
She was in my room

1
Except not a dream but—

8
—really there

5
A fire

2
A campfire

4
Broken glass

1
Bodies in the night

7
Look

8
If I closed my eyes it was like—

5
Burned into my retinas—

3
I was there

1
The greenhouse

2
A party

TEEN CHORUS
A party I had been to

5
There was someone in my room

3
Something

2
Watching me

1
From the darkness

3
I just sat up in bed

7 & 1
Straight up

8
Like I was waiting for it to come back

4 & 3
My skin—

2
The whole time I was thinking about—

4
—tingling

7
Her skin

1 & 2
—those images

3
Why was I thinking about that party?

4
In that flash—

A faint light appears on 10 in the bedroom of 8.

8

Please

It's you, isn't it?

I've heard the rumours

The plague

I don't remember anything, okay?

Nothing

LEAVE ME ALONE!

Please stop looking at me, please, please stop—

Okay I have a—the only memory—

A bird flew into the cafeteria once

A sparrow

It went berserk

Everyone was screaming, laughing, hiding under tables

Throwing balled-up wrappers at it

It kept slamming itself into the big windows over and over again

Lights up faintly on 2.

2

It was not a sparrow, it was in fact a bobolink

It was, in fact, me—trapped in the cafeteria, slamming my body against the glass

I knew it wasn't the way out

But I couldn't find the way out

And I thought, "If I keep slamming myself against this glass"

"maybe they'll understand what I want"

That I need help

That I want out

Out, please

Pick me up—

3

It kept bashing itself against the glass—

2

Pick me up in your hands—

3
—over and over, like it was trying to say—

2
—hold me—

3
—by repeatedly—

2
—my beating heart—

3
—slamming into the glass—

2
—and carry me out

3
—over and over—

2
I will break myself against—

2 & 3
—the glass—

2
Until I lie still
And then, I ask you please
Pick me up in your hands and carry me out

    3 begins to repeatedly run against the wall of the other teens.

3
pick me up in your hands

2
over and over

TEEN CHORUS
bam

2
the glass

3
and carry me out

2
pick me up in your hands

TEEN CHORUS
over and over

2
bam the glass

TEEN CHORUS
and carry me out

3
my beating heart

TEEN CHORUS
and carry me out

2
over and over

3
I will hurt myself until you pick me up and carry me out

3 bursts into tears.

I'm sorry
What happened
That night
It was—
I know—
It was—
We all—
We're all to blame
We said—
We did—
Nothing

Lights shift. Focus on 5.

5
Four o'clock in the morning
My skin crawling, eyes raw
Running
I can hear the buzzer on the kitchen stove going off downstairs
even though I know it's not
I can hear the TV on even though it isn't
The smoke detector
No
The house is silent
Empty
I need to go to sleep
I need to turn off the light
But I know
The second I do, it will return
That something, lurking just out of the corner of my eye

She turns off the light.

Is there someone there?
I can feel you
I know you're there

(screams) Who are you, what do you want?!

    Beat.

I know you're there, Bobbie

    A faint light appears on 10.

10
You've been waiting

5
Waiting?

10
Since the party

5
I barely remember grade nine

10
I was in your class

5
I don't remember you at all

10
I was there a month

5
I don't—

10
Some kids had driven their cars into the field
Had their headlights on
Blasting rap

As she speaks, the field party begins around them—music, dancing, shadows.

I just wandered the crowd
Tried to dance a little

5
Yeah

10
The bonfire

5
A black SUV

10
Whisky shots

5
Headlights and stolen street signs

10
Night danger

5
Bodies in the dark

10
Shadows

5

A boy's stubble
Pine needles in my hair
And sap on my hands

10

I wore a red sweater
Two girls came up to me
They asked me to go with them

5

Were they your friends?

10

I thought maybe
Maybe they would be

5

Who were they?

10

You know them

5

In my school?

10

Yes

5

Tell me

10

You already know

5

Don't go with them
They're not your friends
My dad always said I was a bad seed
Maybe I'm just a bad seed
I once threw a brick through a bay window
My own bay window
Well, my parents were away, and I'd locked myself out
I didn't think to ask the neighbours for a key
Sometimes you don't think
You just throw the brick
It was just like with the sweater
We didn't think
It was just an impulse

Light shift.

10 //
Grade nine.

5
Grade nine

6
First week of school
I found this red sweater

5
You have to understand, this sweater was—

6
I'm not a materialistic person—

5
—perfection

6
—honest—

5
I was there when she bought it

6
But sometimes—

5
Forty per cent off

6
—you find that one that just fits like so perfect, the right colour, the right—

5

—or a style that is you that no one else is wearing

6

And it makes you feel just like so amazing
So I was really excited about this

5

We went back to your place—

6

Made some nachos, put on some music—

5

And we took photos—

6

Just four or five—

5

Really goofing around like—

5 and 6 strike poses.

6

And we post them and I hashtag "newsweater" and everyone's liking it

5

Everyone

6

So everyone knows I've got it and everyone knows—

5

—everyone—

6

—that I'm gonna be wearing it to school the next day

5

You were putting it out there

6

So next day—

5

We're in the caf and—

Cafeteria. 5 and 6 notice 10. She is wearing the same red sweater as 6.

What the fuck?

6

What?

5 indicates 10 across the cafeteria.

Oh
(glances) Whatever
(glances again) Really?
What the fuck?
Is it really the same one?

5

It's the exact same one

6

What should I do?
I don't have anything underneath, I can't even like take it off

5

Since when / does she shop at—?

6
Oh my god, this is mortifying

5
It's not the end of the world

6
We're wearing the exact same fucking sweater

5
It's not so bad

6
Actually I kinda want to die

5
So let's do something about it

6
I mean, I didn't really care

5
We were kind of—

6
Pretending to care—

5
It was mostly just something to get—excited about
Kind of a game

6
I mean, I was totally embarrassed, but I didn't—

5
It wasn't the end of the world

6

Okay, fine, I was a bit pissed off, but it wasn't—

5

—anything like—

6

—that serious

5

I mean looking back it was totally inconsequential

6

It was your idea

5

You dared me to do it

> *5 and 6 pull their chairs over to 10.*

Hey, Billie

10

Oh hi

It's Bobbie, actually

6

Nice sweater

10

I'm sorry, I didn't know—

6

No, that's okay—

10
Forty per cent off—

6
We just wanted to say we think you have like really nice style

5
Seriously

6
Like before we were like, "Who's she again?"

5
But then this morning I was like
"Oh my god, she has your sweater"

10
Oh, well, I wouldn't have bought it if I knew, like, you had it already

6
No, honestly, it's totally cool

10
Cool
Thanks

5
Are you reaching the party tonight?

10
Yeah, I heard about it

6
You should come

10
I don't know—

5
What?

10
I'm not sure it's my thing

5
You drink?

    10 shrugs.

6
Whatever, the three of us will hang out

10
Yeah?

5
For sure

10
It's at the greenhouse, right?

5
Yeah, ten o'clock

6
Please?

10
Well—

6
We can both wear our sweaters

5
Sweater sisters

10
K

6
K, great

5
Sweet

> *Light shift. We are plunged into the chaos of the field party. Music blasts full volume. Shouting. iPhone flashlights streak across the stage. The following lines are sung until the start of 7's monologue.*

1
That night

2
The field

3
The boys

8
Wolf howl

2
Catcall

3
The fire

2
Headlights

1
Fist bump

2
Red cups

8
Roman candle

5, 7, & 8
Fire fight

6
White night

2 & 8
Two-fours

6, 7, & 9
Grade nine

1, 3, 4, 5, & 9
First kiss

2, 3, & 4
Fist fight

1, 4, & 8
Bad fuck

2, 3, & 6
Puking guts

1, 5, & 9
Mouldy couch

3
There was an old couch

2
I remember I passed out

3
Near the greenhouse

2
On this shitty couch

TEEN CHORUS
The old couch
Sees all
She knows all
Oh couch
Great oracle

7 emerges from the chorus as the couch.

7
I used to live in a basement
In one of the nearby homes
I spent about eight or nine years down there
until two boys dragged me into the field
They spent a night drinking beers on me
And then they left me
Other kids would come and lay on me
Smoke or fight or fuck on top of me
When it rained I got bloated
Felt like I was rotting from the inside
Some sort of rodent made a nest inside me

A raccoon, maybe?
It felt big, like a raccoon
I've seen a lot of parties
I was there, the night those girls forced that other girl to walk home naked
Everyone was drunk
But they knew what was happening
And I knew there's no way they would forget
As hard as they tried
And they did
Pretended like nothing had happened
Like it was all cool
But they knew they had crossed a line
And they were trying to erase that line
with more jokes and more beers
People don't take couches very seriously, but I have seen a lot
And I remember everything

> *Blackout. Music blasts. Bodies can be faintly made out moving in the darkness. A few flashes of light from people's iPhones. The sounds of laughter, people shouting each other's names. From the darkness and chaos, lights rise faintly on 5 and 6 as they spot 10 in the party crowd. They descend upon her.*

6
Oh my god, you came, I can't believe you came!

5
And you're wearing the sweater!

10
Yeah
Well
I said I would

6
Fucking great

5
You're so funny

6
Yeah
We like you

10
Yeah?

6
A lot

5
Got good fashion sense
Good sense of humour
Just good senses

6
Common sense

10
I brought some wine
Want some?

5
Cool, thanks

6
You drink?

10
Whatever

5
Fucking whatever's right

6

Does this party suck or what?

10

It's pretty cool

5

Everyone's just like—I don't know

6

Wanna smoke a J in the greenhouse?

5

Oh yeah, let's hit the greenhouse

10

I don't know

6

Are you scared?

5

I got a flashlight on my phone

10

I like the vibe out here

6

She likes the "vibe"

5

C'mon, just for like five minutes

6

Sweater sisters exploration team

5
(laughs) Exploration team?

10
K, but turn on your flashlight

They enter the greenhouse.

6
Have you been in before?

10
Once or twice

6
You're lying

10
Is it safe?

5
Are you the building inspector?

10
Heard a kid got tetanus here once

5
What's that?

6
It's when you step on a nail and you turn into a wolf

10
You come here lots?

6
Oh yeah

5
When we wanna let loose

10
You smoke pot

6
Sometimes

5
Pot's nothing

10
You do like harder stuff?

6
We've got this thing . . . that we do . . .

5
Should we tell her?

6
I don't know

10
What?

5
—way better than pot—

6
But only with our closest friends

10
What is it?

5
I don't know if she's ready

6
You have to promise not to tell anyone

10
I promise

6
We take off all our clothes

5
And we run through the greenhouse

10
Naked?

5
Totally—

6
naked

10
Like totally—

5
Free

10
Isn't it dangerous?

6

Oh my god, / what is with you and the—?

5

—you some kind of danger police?

10

I don't want to step on a bunch of broken glass—

5

You just gotta watch where you're going!

6

But first you have to close your eyes

10

But—

5

That's how it is
We close our eyes

6

Just relax

10

I don't know, I—

5

What?

6

Do you wanna try it or not?

10

I thought we were going to smoke a joint

5
I told you, she's bailing—

6
Lame

10
No, I'm down

6
You sure?

10
Yes

6
Then—close your eyes

5 closes her eyes. Then 6. Then 10.

Keep them closed

5
It's ruined if you open them

6
Totally
Promise?

10
Promise

6
K

5 and 6 open their eyes and suppress giggles.

First, we're all going to pull off our shoes

5
Easy

6
And now our socks
K, next we're going to take off any jewellery we're wearing

5
Even rings?

6
Everything

5
What's next?

6
Now, we take off our shirts
At the same time
No opening your eyes
One, two, three!
Now . . . we're going to take off our pants

10
I knew something bad would happen
But I didn't open my eyes
I listened to the wind rattling the panes of glass above me
Teeth chattering
I needed to believe

5
No peeking!

10

That maybe they really would show me something special at the end
If I just did what they said
Until the end

6

One, two . . . three!

> *5 and 6 grab 10's clothes and run away, full tilt, on "three." 10 is left*
> *standing alone in her underwear.*

10

I didn't need to open my eyes
I knew they'd run away
Taken my shoes so I couldn't chase them

5

We were laughing and running

6

And then—

5

—we weren't laughing, we were just—

6

—running, deeper

5

—than we'd ever gone

6

Into the darkest corner

5

Where the roof had collapsed

6

Her red sweater

5

A bundle

6

Her smell

5

Her body

6

We just let it drop—

5

—as we ran

6

—not even looking at where they fell

10

(*crying*) I remember thinking
the moment before I opened my eyes:
"you're not here"
"This is not really happening to you"
"Erase yourself"
"No one can see you"
"Erase yourself erase yourself"
"erase, erase, erase, erase—"
"If no one can see you, then you're not really naked"
"You're not really alone, they're not really cruel"
and when I opened my eyes I was gone
I wasn't there
I walked slowly over the broken glass
And the broken glass couldn't cut my feet because I had no feet

And I didn't bleed as I walked down the sidewalk
And I wasn't crying as I stumbled out into the field
Past all my classmates by the fire and the couch and the cars
Music playing but no one dancing
Just everyone watching
Staring
Quiet at first
And then someone started laughing

7
It was me
I started laughing

8
Then me

1
Me too

3
I didn't

4
I was—

10
Shivering

4
Speechless

10
My feet cut, bleeding

3

I didn't say anything
I didn't do—

4

—anything

2

Because it was almost like—
We couldn't believe it could ever get to that
Get that bad

7

And none of us wanted to ever feel that

8

And if we said something—

4

—maybe that would be us

10

I walked naked all the way through the field
An airplane passed over like thunder
I erased
Barefoot down the long, twisting street
I erased
The cold asphalt
Passing slowly under the pools of light from the lampposts
I erased each step until I arrived at my front door and I was already gone
And when I transferred schools
when I transferred schools no one even noticed
Because I wasn't
I never was

8
(speaks as fox) I'm nocturnal
So it's very annoying when there are parties in the greenhouse
because it means I have to spend the entire night
hiding in my den, wasting precious hours
I remember that was a particularly bad summer too
Lots of late nights
One morning, when the noise had died away
and the sky was just beginning to brighten
I crept out of my den to look for food
and I came across a pile of clothes
A red sweater and a pair of jeans
I feel sorry for humans
that they don't have fur to keep them warm
They do what they can
but they seem so vulnerable and underprepared
I sniffed the clothes and thought
"Winter's just around the corner"
"I could use something cozy for my den"
So I carried them down into the well
into the basement of the greenhouse
Laid them amidst the sticks and earth
and had my pups on them the next spring

5
The bundle
It really did look like—

6
—a dead body—

5
—lying there like a death

6
A terrible secret

5

That someone was trying to forget

> *Light shift.*

7

That night the shadow passed over

> *Blackout. Music builds. A series of stage images flash before our eyes, punctuating the darkness:*
>
> *1 collapses.*
>
> *8 looks over her shoulder.*
>
> *4 stands downstage smiling from ear to ear in an unnerving manner.*
>
> *7 stands centre stage watching an airplane pass overhead.*
>
> *6 walks in profile to the audience at a glacial pace.*
>
> *Then, from out of the darkness, the bodies of the TEEN CHORUS slowly appear.*

2

I sat up in bed

1

I ran down my stairs and out the door

3

Like a waking dream

7

I knew where I had to go

2

My skin crawling

1

In a flash

4

My blood

1

I ran down the street
My heart pounding
I was awake
I'd never felt more awake

8

We were running

3

We were all

4

Running

2

From the plague

5

Through the streets

3

Jumping fences

1

Towards the field

3
Sleepless

8
Running

7
Until

TEEN CHORUS
All of us

3
Together

6
Back where it had all started

> *In the darkness the* TEEN CHORUS *reprise the medieval choral piece from the prologue. Lights up slowly on 10. She appears naked and cloaked in shadow as she was at the very beginning of the play. Slowly, the teens emerge out of the surrounding shadows. They witness her. Among them are 6 and 5. They step forward and lift 10's clothes out of the well. 5's iPhone tumbles out of the pile of clothes. As they sing 10 takes her clothes back from 6. She dresses in front of them. She stands before them, fully clothed. Blackout.*

Epilogue

9

I'm slated to be torn down next month
So naturally that's put me in a reflective mood
I realize that although this play is named after me
I was basically an impartial bystander
Still, I have a few opinions
I once heard someone say
Ten per cent of any population is cruel, no matter what
and ten per cent is merciful, no matter what
and the remaining eighty per cent can be moved in either direction
Well, I have a lot of hope for the future
I think, by and large, people want to be moved towards mercy
And I think they will
I think we're moving towards mercy

Blackout.

End of play.

Acknowledgements

My deepest, heartfelt thanks to Erin and Cara, for four years of inspiration, collaboration, and friendship.

To all of the teenagers of *Concord Floral* over the years: Mark Correia, Sahra Del, Eslam El-Hamalwy, Theo Gallaro, Eleanor Hart, Erum Khan, Michelle Kuzemczak, Alex Lee, Julian Lee, Eartha Masek-Kelly, Jovana Miladinovic, Samyuktha Movva, Jessica Munk, Micaela Robertson, Troy Sarju, Rashida Shaw, Melisa Sofi, Liam Sullivan, Callum Torrance, Greta Whipple, and Julie Zenderoudi. To all of the friends and collaborators who brought this play to life: Laura Hendrickson, Kimberly Purtell, Christopher Willes, Ravi Jain, Owais Lightwala, Phillipa Croft, William Ellis, Richard Feren, Tye Fitzgerald, Matthew Jocelyn, Sherri Johnson, Kris Knight, Sam Lebel-Wong, Andy McKim, Shawn Micallef, Julian Montague, Natasha Mytnowych, Peter Pasyk, Thomas Payne and Christine Atkinson of LUFF, Rae Powell, Brian Quirt, Naomi Skwarna, Why Not Theatre, the Theatre Centre, Theatre Passe Muraille, Canadian Stage, Nightswimming, Tarragon Theatre, the Linden School, Volcano, Mammalian Diving Reflex, Buddies in Bad Times Theatre, and the Department of Unusual Certainties. To my love, James. And last, but certainly not least, an extra special thank you to Anne Wessels for her generosity and wisdom.

Concord Floral was made possible through the support of the Toronto Arts Council, the Ontario Arts Council, and the Canada Council for the Arts.

Jordan Tannahill is a playwright, author, and director of film and theatre. Jordan's plays have been translated into nine languages and twice honoured with a Governor General's Literary Award for Drama: in 2014 for *Age of Minority: Three Solo Plays* and in 2018 for *Botticelli in the Fire & Sunday in Sodom*. His first novel, *Liminal*, won France's Prix des jeunes libraires, and his second novel, *The Listeners*, was a finalist for the 2021 Giller Prize. In 2019, CBC Arts named Tannahill as one of sixty-nine LGBTQ Canadians, living or deceased, who has shaped the country's history.

First edition: March 2016. Sixth printing: February 2024.
Printed and bound in Canada by Imprimerie Gauvin, Gatineau

Jacket design by Julian Montague
Exterior jacket image elements and interior jacket taken from a photograph
by Erin Brubacher
Author photo © Alejandro Santiago

 PLAYWRIGHTS
CANADA PRESS
202-269 Richmond St. W.
Toronto, ON
M5V 1X1

416.703.0013
info@playwrightscanada.com
playwrightscanada.com